About Starters Facts

This colorful new range of information books encourages young readers to find out things for themselves. The text is graded into three reading levels — red, blue, and green. As well as providing a valuable source of reference, the books encourage further interest in the topic through activities and puzzles.

Accompanying each FACTS book is a STARTERS STORY, which uses the same topic as the starting point for an exciting story.

The STARTERS STORY linked to **Stars**, for example, is a science-fiction adventure, **The Lost Starship**.

Reading Consultants

Betty Root, Tutor-in-Charge, Center for the Teaching of Reading, University of Reading

Geoffrey Ivimey, Senior Lecturer in Child Development, University of London Institute of Education

Stars

illustrated by
Rhoda and Robert Burns

Starters Facts • Green 4

At night we can see the stars. They shine in the dark sky. During the day, the sky is too bright for us to see the stars.
On a clear night, though, we can see hundreds. But there are many more stars which are so faint we can only just see them, and others that are so far away we can't see them at all.

The sun is a star, and it is the nearest
star to us. It is 93 million miles
from the earth. The other stars are much,
much farther away, which is why they look
like tiny points of light. Sometime in
the future, people may travel to the
stars in spaceships.

Orion — the hunter

Cygnus — the swan

Long ago, people who looked at the stars saw that they always stayed in the same patterns. These patterns were called constellations. They were all given names.

The Plough
(Big Dipper)

The Southern Cross

Because the earth goes around, the constellations seem to move through the sky at night. You can see different constellations from different parts of the world. In northern countries you can see the Big Dipper. In southern countries you can see the Southern Cross.

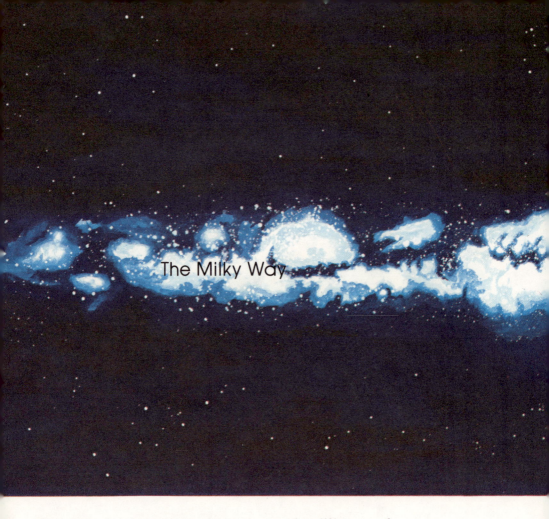

The Milky Way

The sun belongs to a group of millions of stars. This group is called a galaxy. The galaxy that we live in is called the Milky Way Galaxy. There are many other galaxies in space, which are much farther away. The whole of space is called the universe.

This picture shows the whole of the galaxy. The red arrow points to our position in the galaxy.

The universe began thousands of millions of years ago. Some people say that there was a big bang and the galaxies formed. The galaxies moved away from each other, and out into space. The universe is still getting bigger and bigger.

Stars do not last forever. They are born, and they die millions of years later. Stars are made of a gas called hydrogen. The picture shows a cloud of gas, in which new stars are being made.

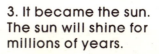
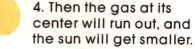

1. The sun began as a cloud of gas floating in space.

2. The middle of the cloud got very hot.

3. It became the sun. The sun will shine for millions of years.

4. Then the gas at its center will run out, and the sun will get smaller.

5. Before the sun dies, it will swell up again.

6. It will get much bigger and become a giant red star. The earth will be burned up.

7. The sun will become so big that it will collapse.

8. The sun will die, and will become a cold, dark object in space.

The sun is an ordinary star. It looks different from other stars because it is so much nearer to us. It will not die for millions of years. Some stars are much bigger and hotter than the sun. They would burn up the earth if they were as near as the sun.

Many stars form in pairs called double stars. Double stars always stay together. There are also groups of stars called star clusters. There is a star cluster in this picture.

An exploding star

Very big stars explode when they die. They become so bright that you can see them during the day. After the explosion, a black hole may be left behind. It is not really a hole, but a small star that sucks in everything around it.

The earth is a planet. Planets are different from stars. Stars are hot, and give out light and heat. Planets are cold. They are lit up by the light from a star. The earth is lit by the sun.

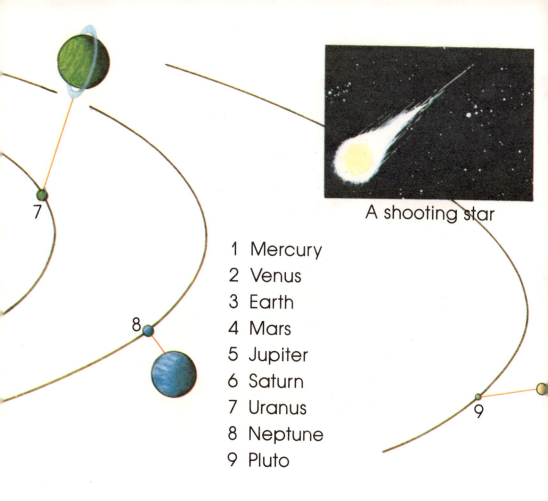

A shooting star

1 Mercury
2 Venus
3 Earth
4 Mars
5 Jupiter
6 Saturn
7 Uranus
8 Neptune
9 Pluto

The earth is not the only planet. Eight more planets go around the sun. Far away in space there may be planets going around other stars.
Sometimes you may see "shooting stars" high in the sky. These are not real stars, but pieces of rock burning in the sky.

Light and heat come through space to us from our star, the sun. We get daytime and nighttime because the world goes around. During the day we face the sun. It is light and may be warm. At night we are turned away from the sun, and it is dark and cooler.

In the summer, the sun often gives us so much light and heat that we can lie on the beach and swim in the sea. Without the sun, it would be so cold and dark that we would die.

Without the sun, plants would not be able to grow. We live by eating plants, or by eating animals that eat plants. Without the sun, we would not have any food. The sun's light and heat also helps to make wood, coal, and oil, which we need for heat and energy.

It is hot in the summer and cold in the winter. This is because the sun is high in the sky in the summer, and low in the sky in the winter. In some places the sun is always high in the sky, so it is always hot. We call these places tropical.

As the earth goes around, the sun seems to move through the sky during the day. You can tell the time by seeing where the sun is in the sky. Do you know how a sundial works?

Once a year on June 21st, which is the first day of summer, the sun rises over the huge stones at Stonehenge.
Stonehenge is an ancient temple in the south of England, built nearly 4000 years ago. It may have been used to work out how the sun moves through the sky.

People who find out about stars are called astronomers. They work in places called observatories. Astronomers look at stars through telescopes. A telescope makes the stars look much brighter. It helps the astronomer find faint stars in the sky.

Stars send out radio waves as well as light rays. Astronomers use radio telescopes to pick up these radio waves. They can find out about stars which are far away in space, and cannot be seen with ordinary telescopes.

Sailors use the sun and stars to find out the position of their ships at sea. They use a sextant to show them how high the sun or stars are in the sky. The sextant helps them to work out where they are.

The sailor is looking at a map of the sea. The sun and the stars help to show him exactly where the ship is. He draws lines on his map — where they cross is the place where the ship is.

Stars Activity

As the sun moves through the sky, it casts shadows on the ground. Get up early on a sunny day, and try making your own sundial — it is very easy!

1. Find a sturdy stick. Make a hole for it in a patch of open ground.

2. The stick will cast a shadow on the ground.

3. Mark the end of the shadow every hour, on the hour.

4. Check the time with a watch, or a clock.

5. Paint the hours on the stones. If the sun goes in, come back another day and fill in the missing hours.

Stars Quiz

These two constellations make pictures in the sky. Trace them out on to paper. Join up the dots. Try to find out their names.

Stars Puzzle

The sailing ship is lost! The Captain does not know which way to go. Can you help him? Which star map should he look at?

Stars Word List

constellation page 4		sundial page 18	
galaxy page 6		temple page 19	
star cluster page 10		astronomer page 20	
planet page 12		radio telescope page 21	
shooting star page 13		sextant page 22	

Each Information book is linked to a story in the new **Starters** program. Both kinds of book are graded into progressive reading levels — red, blue, and green. Titles in the program include:

Starters Facts	Starters Stories
RED 1: Going to the Zoo	RED 1: Zoo for Sale
RED 2: Birds	RED 2: The Birds from Africa
RED 3: Clowns	RED 3: Sultan's Elephants
RED 4: Going to the Hospital	RED 4: Rosie's Hospital Story
RED 5: Going to School	RED 5: Danny's Class
BLUE 1: Space Travel	BLUE 1: The Space Monster
BLUE 2: Cars	BLUE 2: The Red Racing Car
BLUE 3: Dinosaurs	BLUE 3: The Dinosaur's Footprint
BLUE 4: Christmas	BLUE 4: Palace of Snow
BLUE 5: Trains	BLUE 5: Mountain Express
GREEN 1: Airport	GREEN 1: Flight into Danger
GREEN 2: Moon	GREEN 2: Anna and the Moon Queen
GREEN 3: Forts and Castles	GREEN 3: The Secret Castle
GREEN 4: Stars	GREEN 4: The Lost Starship
GREEN 5: Earth	GREEN 5: Nuka's Tale

First published 1981 by
Macdonald Educational Ltd.,
Holywell House,
Worship Street,
London EC2

© Macdonald Educational Ltd. 1981

ISBN 0-382-06561-1
Published in the United States by
Silver Burdett Company
Morristown, New Jersey
1981 Printing

Library of Congress
Catalog Card No. 81-52716

Editor: Philip Steele
Teacher Panel: Susan Alston, Susan Batten, Ann Merriman, Julia Rickell, Gwen Trier
Art Agency: Drawing Attention
Author: Neil Ardley
Production: Rosemary Bishop